Creating Snowflake Art

A Step-by-Step Guide

C. Angela Mohr

Schiffer Publishing Ltd®

4880 Lower Valley Road, Atglen, Pennsylvania 19310

**Other Schiffer Books
on Related Subjects**
*Stenciling:
140 Historical Patterns
for Room Decoration*,
0-7643-0376-7, $24.95

Schiffer Publishing has
a wide variety
of Arts & Craft books.
Please visit our web site
for more great titles.

Photographs by
Kimberly Mohr.

Designed by Stephanie Daugherty
Type set in New Bskvll BT/ New
Bskvll

ISBN: 978-0-7643-2971-5
Printed in China

**Other Schiffer Books
by C. Angela Mohr**

Gourd Puppets and Dolls,
978-0-7643-2868-8, $14.95

Making Gourd Headpieces,
978-0-7643-2869-5, $14.95

Making Gourd Ornaments,
978-0-7643-2716-2, $12.95

Gourd Art Basics,
978-0-7643-2829-9, $14.95

Schiffer Books are available at special discounts
for bulk purchases for sales promotions or premiums.
Special editions, including personalized covers,
corporate imprints, and excerpts can be created in
large quantities for special needs. For more information
contact the publisher:

Published by Schiffer Publishing Ltd.
4880 Lower Valley Road
Atglen, PA 19310
Phone: (610) 593-1777;
Fax: (610) 593-2002
E-mail: Info@schifferbooks.com

For the largest selection of fine reference
books on this and related subjects, please
visit our web site at
www.schifferbooks.com
We are always looking for people
to write books on new and related
subjects. If you have an idea for a
book please contact us at the
above address.

This book may be purchased from the publisher.
Include $3.95 for shipping.
Please try your bookstore first.
You may write for a free catalog.

In Europe, Schiffer books are
distributed by
Bushwood Books
6 Marksbury Ave.
Kew Gardens
Surrey TW9 4JF England
Phone: 44 (0) 20 8392-8585;
Fax: 44 (0) 20 8392-9876
E-mail:w
info@bushwoodbooks.co.uk
Website: www.bushwoodbooks.co.uk
Free postage in the U.K., Europe;
air mail at cost.

Contents

Dedication

This book of snowflake papercuttings is dedicated to my brother, Robert, who would rather be skiing than most anything else. Robert works like a pack animal making things happen for his family and friends, and if you are fortunate to have him in your circle, laughter and good storytelling is never far away. Robert is a true sparkle on the snowbank of life and I am fortunate to have him as one of my brothers!

A Flurry of Information

Folding paper and papercutting have been around for thousands of years in various forms. Every culture has its own tradition of paper arts: folded origami designs of China, colorful layered wycinanki of Poland, symmetrical scherenschnitte of Germany, and French silhouettes. The Jewish culture has a long history of papercuttings based on religious symbols and spiritual traditions still practiced today especially wedding contracts, ketubahs. Mandalas are familiar to many cultures for their circular designs and traditional meanings of universe and spirituality.

Who were the first to start cutting snowflakes? I suspect the practice is indigenous to any culture with a papercutting tradition, whether they lived in cold climates with snow or not because a snowflake is the generic term used for a design cut repetitively in a circular format, either as a flat piece of paper or by folding the paper and cutting multiple layers at one time. With this thought in mind, snowflakes can be designed with any theme to make remarkable gifts, ornaments, or decorating items.

There are many diverse and interesting books currently on the market laying out patterns for snowflake images. They are handy snatches when a papercutter wants to get the job done. But what if you want something special, something original?

Like most people, you probably cut snowflakes in school for some kind of project or bulletin board. I remember being handed construction paper and a pair of 'safety scissors' when I was in elementary school. I was instructed to fold the paper this way and that way to produce a wedge shape and then cut bits and pieces out of the sides. The result was clumsy and awkward. The paper was wrong, the scissors were wrong, and after a while, my attitude was wrong. (*GASP!*) A successful project begins with a higher level of equipment and certainly different kinds of paper. In the next section, I provide some examples of tools and papers that I have found helpful for designing and cutting original snowflakes.

Chapter One

Equipment

Cutting Tools

The actual cutting tool you use will depend on the number of layers to be cut. The more layers, the sharper the tool needs to be, broadly speaking. Generally, snowflakes cut from regular copier-weight paper need to be 6-point or less so that the layers are workable. A higher number of snowflake points are beautiful, but would require an Xacto knife with a #11 blade to cut intricate details. A lighter weight paper, such as tissue paper, can be folded into more layers and doesn't need a knife. Different papers, differing number of layers to be cut—these are the factors that determine the tool.

The same is true with scissors or hole punchers. The paper's weight will determine what *KIND* of scissors or hole punchers you use as well. Scissors came in all sorts of sizes and levels of sharpness. Try to use what you already have on hand and then, after cutting several designs with them, try a different pair. Notice the differences.

I use Ultra-Fine Revlon curved-tip cuticle scissors. I have friends who buy surgical scissors or special scherenschnitte scissors from Europe (which are fabulous!), but I like being able to run out to the local pharmacy and picking up extra pairs for about $10. Then, if I drop them or ruin them somehow, it's no biggee. If I lose or ruin a pair of really nice scissors, my heart is breaking!

Within the last several years, a whole new market for hole punchers and designer-edge scissors has opened. Sometimes the best way to handle a design is using these in combination with scissors or a knife. I'm not advocating a rush to purchase a rack of new tools, but they may be handy if you have already invested.

Some equipment to use for papercutting would be cuticle scissors, regular scissors, hole punchers, pencil, stencils, copier paper, origami paper, wrapping paper, silhouette paper, glue stick, darning needle, glue.

Paper

Paper can be a real sticking point for a lot of people. There are purists who say that papercuttings, because they are lightweight, should only be cut from archival papers (non-acid) so that they last generations. I agree with the "lasting" part, but papercutting is a simple skill, meant to be basic. Our ancestors did not have access to all the archival wares we do today, and many papercuttings have survived hundreds of years. Most damage done to papercuttings happens from improper and constant exposure to the sun or moisture. Be open to the paper you use. The best paper for your project might be right next to your hand and, (*gulp!*), not be archival!

I use giftwrap, origami, silhouette, copier, and scrapbook papers. Giftwrap and origami papers are good for detailed snowflake papercuttings. Copier and scrapbook papers are sturdier and suitable for ornaments or bulletin boards. Scrapbook papers, like origami paper, come in a square format. Since snowflakes are based on a circle cut from a square, some of your effort is already done. If the

Fold one corner to the opposite side of the paper.

Align the two sides...

...and crease the fold.

The leftover paper beyond the triangle is cut off with scissors or an Xacto knife.

Unfold the triangle for a square.

This works for all sizes of paper.

Chapter Two

Folding & Cutting Paper

The beauty of a circular design is the symmetry, which means snowflakes have an even number of points: 4, 6, 8, 12, and so forth. The higher the number of points, the more folds there will be and therefore the more layers to cut through.

When cutting many layers, you want to avoid 'creep': the phenomenon of paper sliding against paper as the scissors move through the layers. You can think you are cutting a nice line, only to find out at the end that the paper has shifted completely out of alignment, altering the design. The more layers, the more creep will happen. That is why it is a good idea to stabilize a wedge of folded paper with staples, or if you really want a complicated design, use the Rotating Slice strategy we will review later. Here are some examples of different layer thickness and creep:

Here are some wedges of paper, folded for snowflake cutting. Notice how the wedges of folded paper have been trimmed across the top to eliminate the pointy tails of the beginning square, and how the choice of paper changes the thickness of the wedge that has to be cut.

See how the paper in this wedge is shifting out of alignment as the scissors move through the many layers.

When the snowflake is opened, you can see part of the design has been cut so thin that it might fall off!

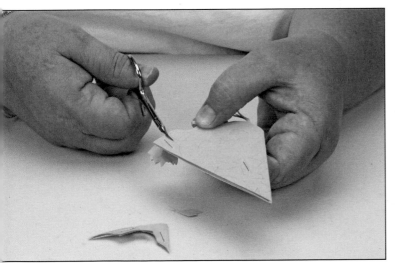

Stapling the wedge in the open areas of the design (the parts that will be cut away anyway) keeps the paper still...

...so when the snowflake is opened, everything is intact.

When finished cutting, ironing the snowflake between two pieces of baking parchment helps erase fold lines. Pressing the snowflake in a large book works well too (over time!), but remember which book you put the snowflake in so you can retrieve it later.

A snowflake is put on a piece of baking parchment. I finger-press any small details flat.

Cover with another piece of parchment, making sure all the ends and tails and pieces have not folded but are flat.

Move a hot iron across the top piece of parchment in a circular fashion, keeping in constant movement so no one spot gets scorched.

Most of the folding lines will be flat, as will fine lines or details.

Quarter Folds

A quarter fold is folding the paper in four equal sections. This fold is good as a start for 4, 8, and 16 points, depending on how many times the paper is folded in half. I like it for 8-point snowflakes, which is a good number for cutting if the paper is thin enough for my scissors to handle the layers. Plus, the starburst is interesting without getting too busy the way 16 points can.

It starts with folding a paper square in half:

Fold the paper so that the corners meet, aligning the sides.

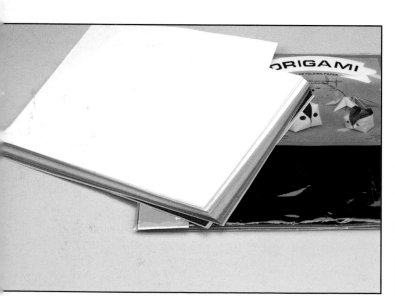

We will use 8" or 10" squares of copier and origami papers.

Crease the fold sharply to make a rectangle.

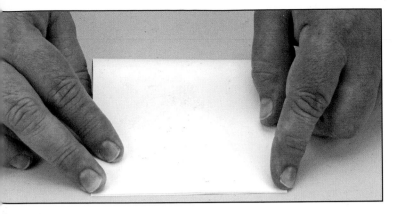

Fold the paper again so the corners from one short side meet the corners on the opposite side, making a square.

This made a wedge for a 4-point snowflake.

As the folds become bulky, the paper will resist. Roll the folded edge with a pencil to loosen the paper fibers.

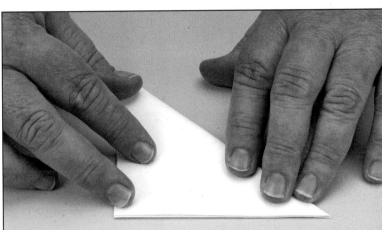

Refold the paper as before, and turn one folded side of the wedge over to align with the other folded side and crease.

Crease the fold sharply. As the layers build, running the side of a pencil over the fold makes a satisfying crease.

Open to see how this was a wedge for an 8-point snowflake. For demonstration purposes, I have cut a curve at the open end of the wedge to emphasize the points.

Refolding the wedge and making one more fold (carefully, because at this point the paper is going to rebel)...

No matter how many points you are trying to achieve, accurate folding and creasing will form the foundation of accurate snowflake papercuttings. If the folded wedge of paper is loose, or misaligned, the design will not be as recognizable as it could have been.

...makes a wedge for a 16-point snowflake. You probably wouldn't have a snowball's chance of cutting through a wedge like this, but the folded lines can serve as guides for tracing elaborate designs.

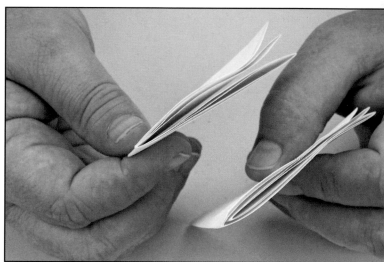

When folding the paper for your snowflake papercutting, make sure all your folds are tightly packed into each other.

Triple Folds

Triple folds produce 6- and 12-point snowflakes. Six-point snowflakes are the ones you are probably familiar with from your school days since they had the least amount of layers to cut yet still maintained a visually interesting starburst effect. Triple folds start with folding paper in half, either horizontally or diagonally:

Right: **Fold the paper in half as before, or fold diagonally by turning one corner of the square of paper toward the directly opposite corner so the edges on either side of the corners align. I'll do both versions so you can see the results.**

Crease the folds sharply.

Open to see the pinch mark.

The goal is to divide your folded paper into thirds. Bend the folded edge over as if you are going to fold it in half...

Using the center mark, fold one side of center past the mark to divide the paper into thirds...

...and make a small pinch to mark the center of the folded edge.

...and lightly tap the new fold. This fold will be temporary until we know the other side works.

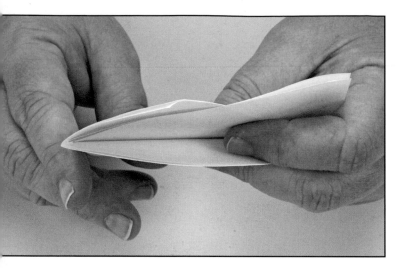

Fold the other side of center past the center mark to be snugly on top of the first, and tap another temporary fold. The interior fold should nest tightly inside the exterior fold.

Once the thirds have been refolded and everything aligns properly...

The edges should align. Oops!

...crease all folded edges sharply.

If not, open the wedge and reposition.

When you open this wedge, you see the makings of a 6-point snowflake.

Another fold of the same wedge will make the foundation for a 12-point snowflake.

Rotating Slice

If a person took a slice of dessert from a precut pie, all the other slices would still look like the slice that was plated. That is the basis for the Rotating Slice strategy. This can be used when you need to reduce the number of paper layers to cut at once or the design is delicate and needs a careful touch.

To use this strategy, you will be folding the paper into quarter or third folds and using the folded edges as guidelines for tracing the slice's design.

Let's try a slice of something and see what all this means.

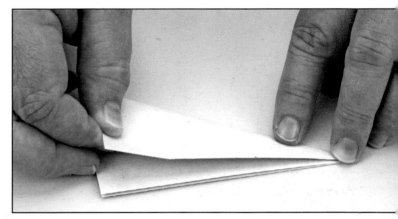

Fold the paper into a wedge for a 12-point snowflake.

Let's say you want to do a 12-point snowflake with apples for a project about the 12 months of the year. Cutting through 12 layers of paper will not be successful, but six layers is do-able. So, select your apple images.

To make a slice of art, arrange an apple on a piece of paper the same size as the wedge.

Make sure the apple touches the sides of the paper, and trace the outline.

Add detail to the empty areas. Since apples are historically the fruit of love, knowledge and abundance, I am adding a heart and a seed with lines connecting the three images together.

Cut out the art so it becomes a template you can use to rotate from one side of the wedge to the other.

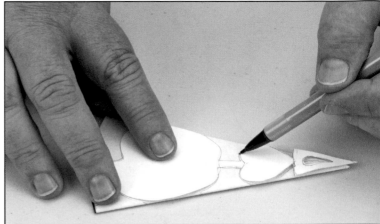

Position the slice of art on the wedge and trace.

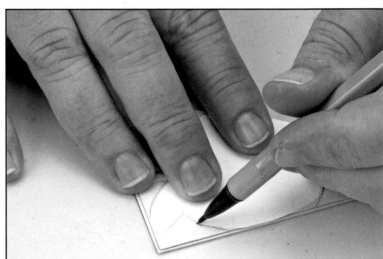

Rotate to the other side of the wedge and repeat the tracing.

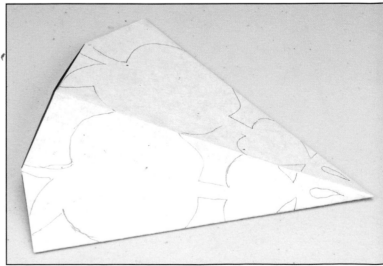

Now, open the snowflake one time...

...and cut as if you are cutting a 6-point snowflake. Start with the interior areas, then the side, and finally the top edge. Hold the scissors hand and arm in one position, and move the paper into the scissors.

When finished, open the snowflake to see 12 apples and you only had to cut through 6 layers of paper.

To make a poster board snowflake, get a piece of regular paper the same size as you want the finished snowflake to be. Fold it into a wedge for a 6-point snowflake.

Unfold the wedge and flatten the paper enough to sit on the poster board, but still have the fold lines evident.

Make small, insignificant marks at the end of each of the fold lines.

Connect the marks on opposite sides of the snowflake with a light pencil line, moving through the center.

Now you have six slice areas to put the piece of art you want to use.

Cut out the design to make a template, or slice of art.

Go back to the paper you folded for the poster board and cut out one of the folded slices.

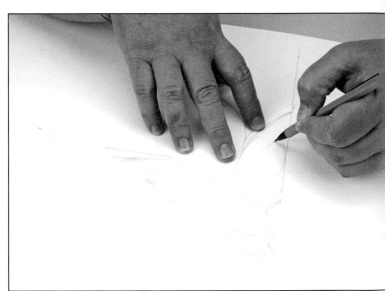

Position the slice of art onto one of the poster board slices and trace carefully.

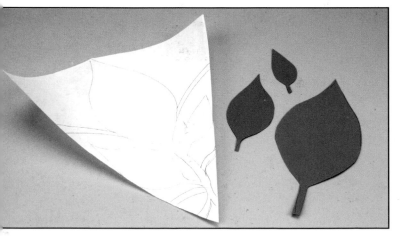

Arrange images on the paper so they touch the sides. These touches are where the art will connect one area to another on the poster board. I am using leaves and stems.

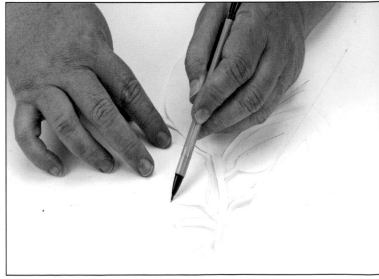

Go to another slice and do the same.

18

Review your first two slices to make sure the slices of art are meeting at the fold lines. If not, make adjustments to the art before continuing. All the slices should meet at the fold lines so they connect when the snowflake is done. If so, continue all around the snowflake. Be sure to make the same adjustments after tracing each slice.

After tracing the slice of art all around the snowflake, put the poster board on a safe cutting surface and use an Xacto to cut all the lines. Pull the knife toward you.

Here is the finished poster board snowflake!

19

Putting Together a Design

Here are some designs I made. I refolded the snowflakes and put them all on the copier glass to get a record of them for future use.

As stated earlier, there are many snowflake pattern books available for a great, quick project. However, when you want something original, something unique, it is worth a little extra thought to make your own design. An original snowflake takes just as long to cut as a pattern, but is much more satisfying because you can include personal details. Also, by producing original designs, you actually make a pattern book of your own...to be sure to keep a copy of the designs you invent!

Geometric designs

Geometric designs are the basic snowflake images most folks remember. Made of triangles, squares, and circles, these are the snowflakes from childhood. Use templates to build a design: cookie cutters, drafter's tools, or various buttons. These designs do not require anything but a willingness to combine shapes. Try tracing household items like trivets to get a design onto a wedge of folded paper. Dropping several buttons onto a wedge and tracing them, in combination with some connecting lines, can make lovely original snowflake papercuttings. If you do not particularly like the paper you chose, spray paint it!

Let's use some of these ideas:

Right: **I am using papers folded for 6- and 8-pointed snowflakes.**

For this one, we'll use a template available at craft stores. Start at the center and make a circle.

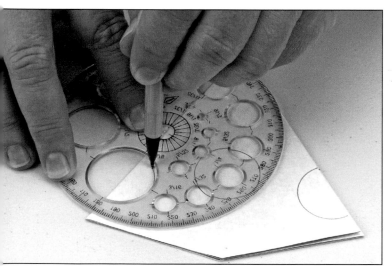

Above the circle, on either side, add two half circles on the fold. The half circles on a fold will become a full circle once the snowflake is opened.

Below the center circle, on either side, add a half square on the fold.

Make one V shape at the point. Notice how we've gone from 3 shapes at the top, to 2 shapes at the middle, to 1 at the point. 3,2,1…a rhythm. That is part of designing, establishing a rhythm of shapes.

Add connecting lines so everything is attached to each other somehow. I will use straight lines like Tinker Toys.

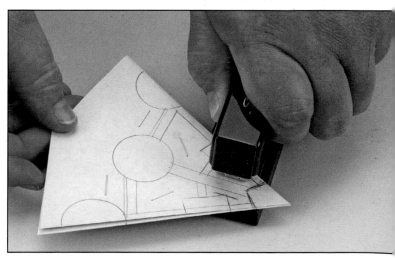

To reduce creep, stabilize the design by stapling the empty areas that will be cut away.

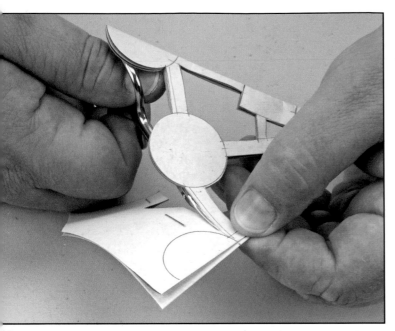

Cut the design.

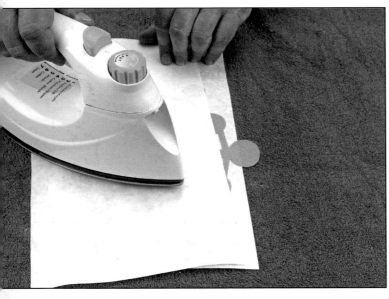

Open the snowflake and iron flat between pieces of parchment paper.

For a totally random design, drop some buttons onto a wedge.

Trace the shapes. A couple shapes I am making into flowers.

For connecting lines, I am adding curved lines this time because I already chose to do the flower thing. Another part of designing: once you set a course, stick with the plan. That way, all the components reflect a consistent thought.

Add leaves to the curved lines. Again, maintaining the previously chosen path.

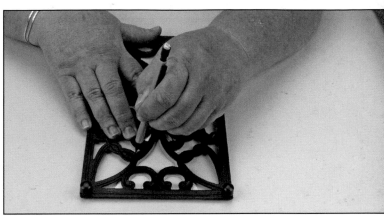

For this wedge I am tracing a metal trivet. Metal work makes lovely designs!

Cut out the design.

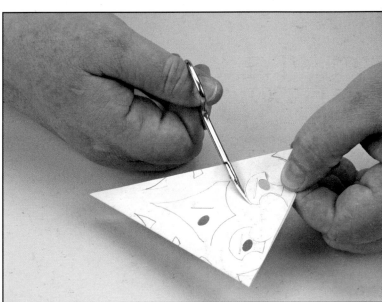

Cut. To get inside a tight place, a hole puncher can be use to make the initial opening, then the scissors will do their job without ripping the paper.

Open and iron.

Open and iron.

Here is a snowflake I made with some paper I thought was going to be great, but it turned out the printed design on the paper fights with the art I cut.

So, I ironed the snowflake as flat as I could, then used spray paint to make a uniform color. The design became instantly evident.

Free-Hand

I'm not going to lie to you and say anyone can draw free-hand because that just is not true. However, if you can draw and have some idea of the theme you want to celebrate, figure out three or four suitable images. A simple drawing is all you need, just the silhouette. Once done, fit the images onto a folded paper wedge making sure the edges of the silhouette overlap the folded edges of the paper. If the first attempt does not work well enough to suit you, decide where to make a change and start over. It is just paper you know! Have some fun and be inventive. That's all you need to create something original.

Let's walk through an example:

We will use a cupcake and big candle instead of a big cake and fifty candles. We can place his initial R on either side of the candle.

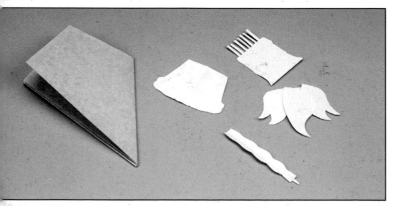

For example, let's say we're making a birthday snowflake for Robert, who is turning 50 years old. Here are the images we will arrange on a wedge of folded paper for an 8-point snowflake.

We will put the number 50 in the flame and at the base of the cupcake, and the initial becomes a ribbon line holding the cupcake, candle, and flame together as one unit.

Staple the wedge of paper to stabilize.

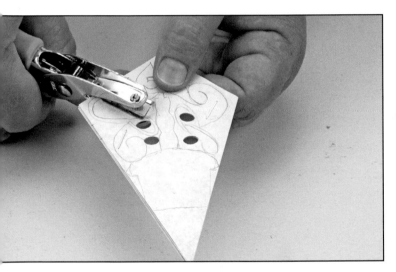

Use hole punchers to start cutting the interior spaces.

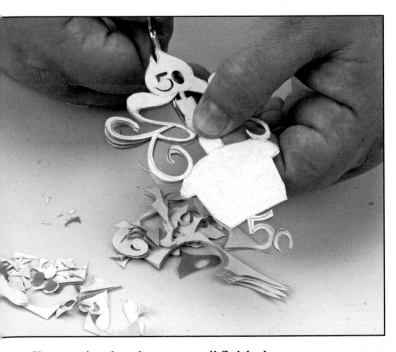

Keep cutting the other parts until finished.

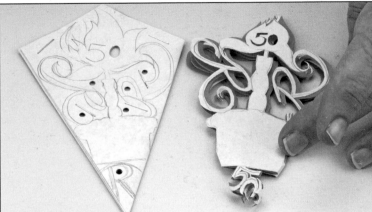

Open and have a look. This would be the time to re-arrange the design and retrace onto a new wedge of folded paper if we thought of a better idea or wanted to make anything bigger or smaller. I think more flame is needed since the old boy is 50.

I retraced to shorten the candle and make the cupcake smaller so there is room for more flame. I also changed the bottom 50 under the cupcake to the letter "R."

Re-cut.

Once done and opened, I will iron flat before framing.

Copyright-Free

Copyright-free images are pieces of art that have reached their 'expiration date' or have been offered for use with permission. Copyright-free sources will always indicate permission status, so if the book or online source has not mentioned permission specifically, it is better to assume the artist still has ownership of the art. *BUT*, if the images are free for use, they can be a handy beginning for altered or new images. This can be a fun way to make meaningful and interesting original snowflakes. Dover Publications is a widely known producer of copyright-free images for artists and crafters. Here are examples of how to play with freebies:

Left: Here are some Dover books with copyright-free images we can use to personalize. There are silhouette books, typography books, and books with borders. They have a wealth of starting images we can play with to show how to combine and alter for personal use.

Gather some images, a piece of paper the same size as the wedge of folded paper we'll use for our snowflake, and the wedge of folded paper.

Cut out the design...

Arrange the images on the paper so they touch the sides. If you want to alter the images to make an original piece, do that before you arrange them on the paper.

...and use it as a template to trace onto the wedge of folded paper

Cut out the design.

Open and iron.

Image Orientation

The way a design is oriented on the folded wedge of paper for a snowflake will determine the overall effect once the folded paper is opened. When looking at a wedge of folded paper, notice that the line between the center of the top edge and the main point is shorter than the line between the two corners and the main point. Knowing this difference matters when you want to accent one particular part of a design. Depending on how the images are placed on the wedge of folded paper, completely different results can be had. This can be handy when you need to make similar, but different, snowflakes for several people. The following process will show how easy it is to be original:

First, I redraw the girl so the pumpkin is a box with a bow, her hair is long, and the dress bow is bigger. I make the silhouette simple.

I want to make a wedding snowflake of a girl carrying a present. Here is a pilgrim girl carrying a pumpkin. Watch how the snowflake changes depending on the orientation of a silhouette of this image.

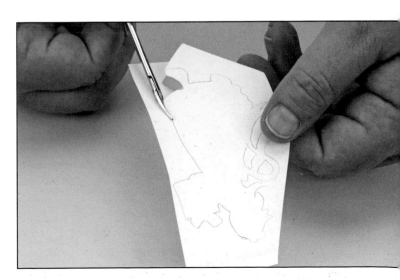

I cut out the new piece of art. It will be traced in different ways onto several wedges of folded paper.

27

On this first version, she is centered on this wedge with extra ribbons on the box.

Here, I put two girls on a wedge. One girl is positioned so the middle of the box is on the folds, and the other girl is behind her. I place a bow at the ground beneath their feet.

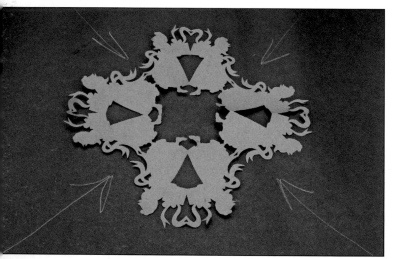

When I cut it out and opened it, I thought the design was lacking in four places.

This wedge was opened and the girl traced onto each slice separately because we want to have her walking in the same direction all around the snowflake. This snowflake will be cut as a single layer without folding.

After I added a heart to the empty area and retraced onto a new wedge, it turned out much nicer! Don't be afraid to fail and back up for another try – in fact, that's a good lesson for life.

Cut out the design.

Don't forget the center!

Iron it flat.

See how the same image oriented in different positions can give totally different finished looks.

Chapter Four

Blizzard of Projects

Now you have enough basic snowflake knowledge to start designing your own personal snowflakes. At first, folks are intimidated by the idea of designing their own snowflakes until an event arrives to test their imagination. These projects show there is no "correct way" to achieve a lovely papercutting. All were born of celebrating family and friends' happy times.

Let's be original!

Door Wreaths

I have a glass storm door at my front entrance and, although it is very nice for deterring weather from the house's interior, the space between it and the front door is so small I cannot hang a traditional wreath on my front door. This is where a papercutting is great—and a snowflake is fabulous! It is round, so top-to-bottom orientation is not an issue as the door opens and closes and moves a little. And, it is visually interesting from the street when the color contrasts with the color of the door.

Using leaves on a wedge will produce an interesting autumn wreath. We'll use maple leaves here. Because the paper is printed with autumn leaves and kind of busy visually, as you'll see, we will be straightforward in our placement so our design does not fight with the paper.

Cut out the design and open.

Iron it flat.

Use a glue stick to attach it to a piece of poster board.

...and hang!

Use an Xacto knife to cut the poster board about a half inch around the outer edge of the snowflake.

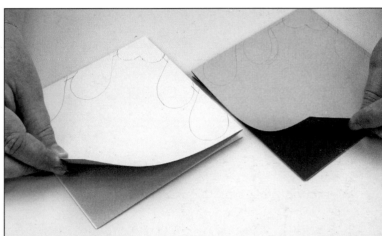

Here are two wedges of folded paper with heart designs. These wedges are folded to make a 4-point snowflake. For demonstration purposes, I am using two-sided paper.

Duct tape a string onto the top area of the back...

Cut the two heart snowflakes.

31

Open them and iron flat.

Attach a loop on the back of one of the heart points and hang.

Use double-stick tape to attach narrow strips of foam core board or other stiff board to the backs of both snowflakes.

Family initials make a friendly and eye-catching welcome at the front door. We will be using foam core as a sturdy base for this wreath but to start, let's make a large wedge by folding a 24" piece of paper to make a large 6-point snowflake.

Position one snowflake over the other and double-stick the centers together.

I chose the initials L and M from a copyright-free type book. They were enlarged and arranged to fit the large format of the wedge we folded. Notice the L has been cut and spaced a little so the bottom part reaches both sides of the paper.

Once the design was settled, I cut out the initials...

...then trace the template onto the wedge.

Cut out the initials making a large, but flimsy snowflake.

Place the snowflake onto the foam core board.

To keep the snowflake from shifting, choose 3 or 4 places toward the center where double-stick tape can easily be put on the back and pressed into place. Working in a circular fashion, apply double-stick tape to the back of the snowflake.

Trim the foam core board.

Duct tape a loop on the back and hang.

Pencil a simple design around the edge of the wedge since the center will not have art.

Doilies

Doilies are nothing more than snowflakes with something sitting on their centers! Actually, they are circular edge papercuttings cut from snowflake-folded papers. Coffee filters make terrific absorbent doilies, parchment paper is good for sticky treats, and holiday giftwrap snowflakes serve as colorful plate or candle chargers. Here we go:

Cut and use.

Coffee filters are easy to cut. Iron them flat to begin then fold into a wedge.

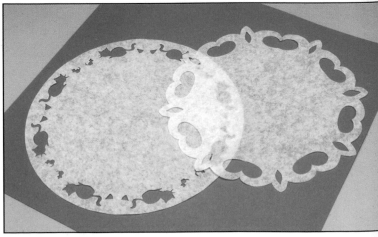

Here are some fun designs.

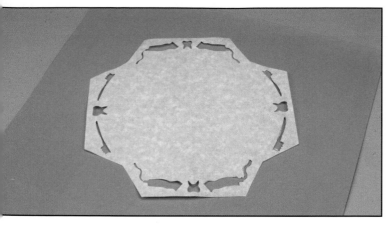

Baking parchment makes a good doily for sticky treats. This one has a design of toothpaste and toothbrushes for a plate of sugary treats — a devilish maneuver to make a statement!

Fold a 6" square of gold wrapping paper for a 12-point snowflake by folding in half to make a rectangle...

...in half again to make a square...

...in half again on the diagonal...

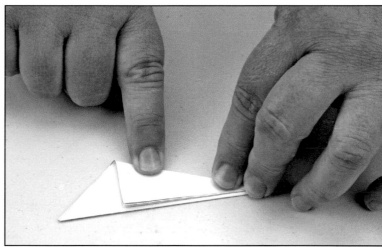

...and once again on the diagonal.

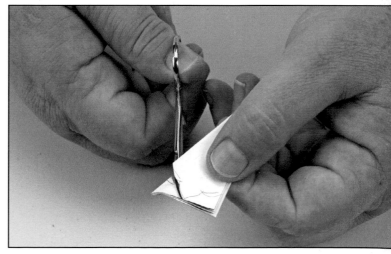

Use scissors to cut the top edge into two humps with a pointed oval in the middle.

Open the snowflake by one fold...

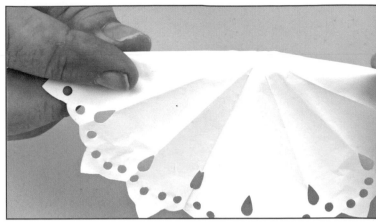

Open the whole snowflake and re-crease the folds so they all bend backwards, toward the back.

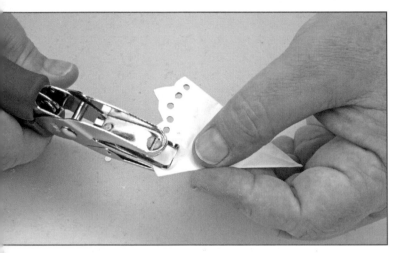

...and hole punch a line of holes under the top edge with a hole puncher.

Open the snowflake by one more fold and make another line of holes using a puncher with a different design.

Hold the middle area of the snowflake against the bottom of a taper. Mold the snowflake around the base of the taper and fit it into a candlestick.

Bulletin Board Big

Bulletin boards are big areas needing visual interest fast. Snowflakes can be the simple way to use up space with something interesting to look at and ponder. They can also be meaningful ways to highlight an event subject, like President's Day or classroom birthdays. If you are at a school with large rolls of construction paper, you are in luck! If not, use rolls of butcher paper or wrapping papers for large pieces of paper.

Arrange the images so the edges touch the folded sides and trace. Notice I've made the flag and star bigger.

Designing for a bulletin board is easy because the images are big enough to cut around with regular scissors. For a Presidents' Day snowflake we will use this silhouette of George Washington, Abraham Lincoln, a flag, and a star.

Cut.

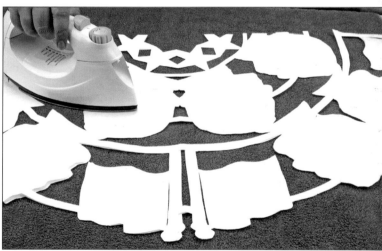

Unfold and iron out creases. Here it is only open to half size.

Fold a really large piece of paper to fit the bulletin board into a wedge shape for an 8-pointed snowflake. This piece was 36" square.

Create add-ons such as a top hat and beard for Lincoln, a bow for George, and some stars for the flag. Make sure to cut as many add-ons as you have snowflake folds.

Chapter Five

Finishing Techniques

Ornaments

Hanging ornaments are made with two snowflake papercuttings. I use stiff paper for hanging ornaments because they will get hard wear from repeated use. Cover stock used for greeting cards is good, or perhaps inexpensive paper plates. Since these kinds of paper can be too stiff to fold successfully, I fold only once and then use the rotation technique to achieve the snowflake design. After the snowflakes are cut, they are attached to each other.

Let me show you three ways:

Cut two 6-point snowflakes with flat, uncut areas of paper. Notice the center fold area has not be cut.

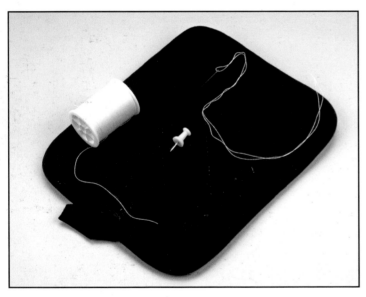

To sew two snowflakes together by hand, get a potholder, a push-pin, a needle, and thread.

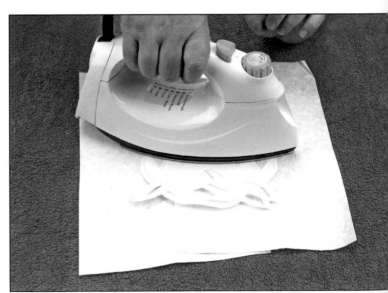

Open and iron flat.

Situate the two snowflakes on the potholder so the folds sit on top of each other.

Using a pushpin, puncture holes ¼" apart along the center fold.

Thread a needle with a 24" double thread. Knot the ends together.

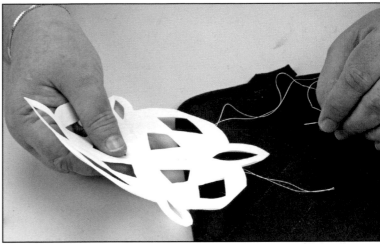

Put the needle and thread into the top hole, and pull it through to leave a 4" tail of thread.

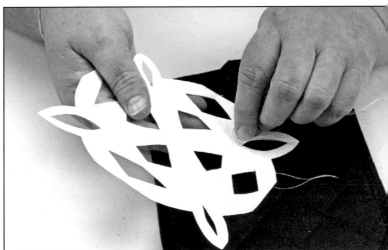

Go into the next hole.

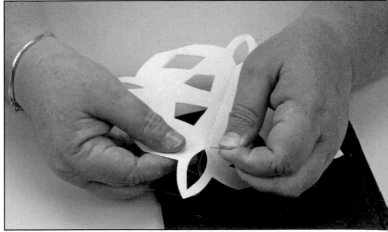

Continue sewing in and out of the holes along the center fold until you reach the bottom.

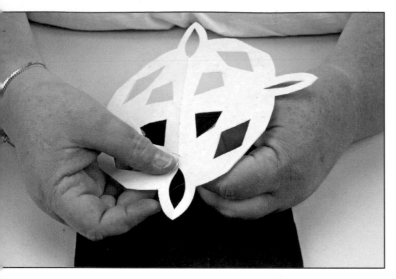

At the bottom, turn the snowflake over and continue sewing up the same line of holes to the end.

At the top, tie a double knot at the snowflake edge...

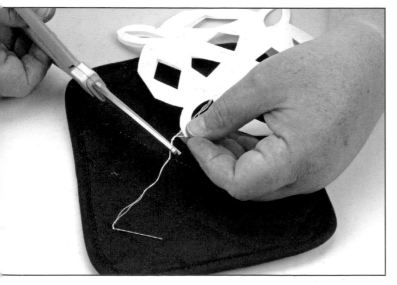

...and another one 4" from the edge. Trim the extra thread.

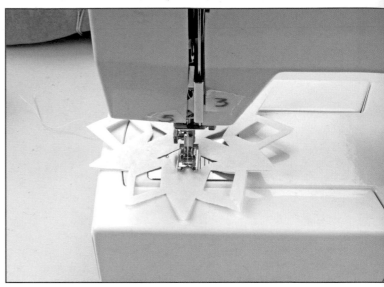

OR, to machine sew, cut two snowflakes as before but put them together under the foot of the sewing machine, leaving several inches of thread hanging, and sew to the end.

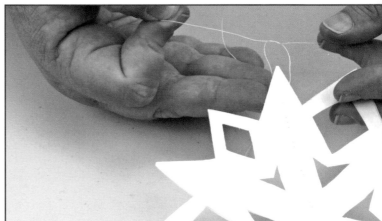

Tie knots in the threads at both ends.

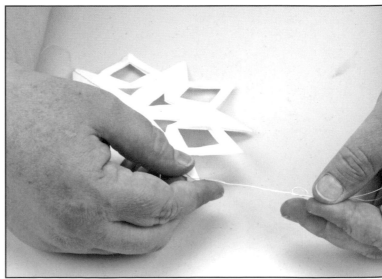

Tie a knot in the thread about 4" from the top of the snowflake.

Whether hand- or machine-sown, fold the snowflake arms outward to make a 3-dimensional ornament.

Slide the snowflakes together by pushing the slits against each other.

To avoid having to sew heavy paper like poster board, cut a slit in both snowflakes halfway along the center fold.

Once in position, let dry thoroughly.

Apply a thin layer of glue along the slits.

A piece of thread can be used for hanging.

Framed Art

Sometimes I just want to make a lovely, meaningful gift for a wedding, a significant birthday, or a house-warming gift. Because this kind of snowflake will be framed, I can use a more elaborate design and delicate paper. Origami paper is delicate, as are some wrapping papers. I choose paper and images suitable to the event and the people involved. Square frames are hard to find readily. They can be made at a framing shop, or you can use display frames for record album covers. We'll start by attaching the snowflake to a backing:

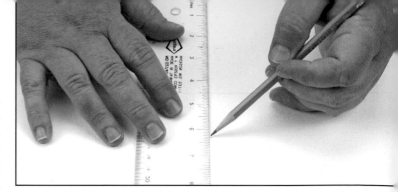

Find center, top-to-bottom and side-to-side. The center of the snowflake will be positioned just above this mark. Note: For something to be centered in a frame optically, it has to be technically a breath higher than center.

To prepare a papercutting for framing, it needs to be secured to a backing. Choose a sturdy paper to be the backing for your snowflake.

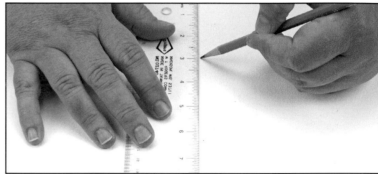

Mark discreet dots every couple inches vertically above and below the center mark.

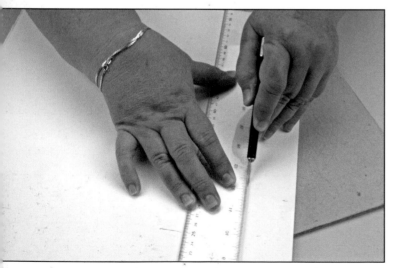

Cut the backing to fit your frame.

Orient the snowflake so that it is a breath higher than the center, using the center dot as your point of reference.

Making sure the snowflake doesn't shift, put a tiny drop of glue on the back of one area of the snowflake and let fall into place.

Choose another area, carefully lift it, and place a tiny drop of glue on the back.

Do this same procedure with other areas of the snowflake. Because the cutting will be in a frame for protection, it will not need every area completely glued to the backing.

While the glue dots you have done are drying, carefully erase the center dot if it is visible.

After the glue has dried and the snowflake is not going to shift, try to lift the edges to check for any areas where an additional dot of glue would be handy.

Add a dot or two of glue where needed.

Keep checking for large, loose areas. Touch discreet dots of glue to these areas. Remember, tiny dots of glue—just enough to hold it without being too bulky and obvious.

Once the glue is dried, make sure the frame glass is clean and free of lint.

Scoop up all layers into the frame.

Layer the following items: the frame's backing board, several layers of paper, the cutting now attached to its backing, and the glass. The several layers of paper acts as a buffer between the art and the framing.

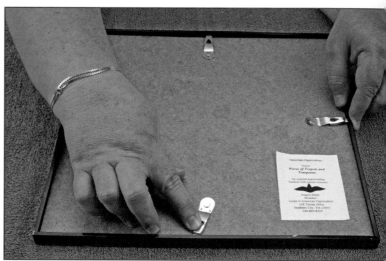

Turn the frame over and use the tension clamps provided to secure your artwork into the frame.

Position the frame over the layers.

Pretty! Use double stick tape to attach a card or paper with the title of the snowflake, who designed and cut it (you!), what occasion it celebrates, and the month and year.

 Conclusion

By now you probably have a head full of ideas! Make sure to cut the first try of a new idea from a piece of scrap paper. That will orient you to any tricky corners or cold spots. Once you get the design to your liking, go to the better paper. Keep in mind, even at the 'final stage', there can, and will, be changes. That is the fun and infinite joy of original papercutting!

As you discover the lasting thrill of unfolding original snowflakes, I heartily encourage you to share the delight with others! Investigate the world of papercutting by becoming a member of the Guild of American Papercutters. Go online to the Guild's website at www.papercutters.org and join the conversation in the Community. The Guild sponsors an open environment for anyone, member or not, to meet and learn from other papercutters around the country. Find out for yourself how interesting and diverse papercutting enthusiasts can be!

Gallery

54